T0179996

A Note from
Mary Pope Osborne About the

MAGIC
TREE HOUSE®
FACT TRACKERS

When I write Magic Tree House® adventures, I love including facts about the times and places Jack and Annie visit. But when readers finish these adventures, I want them to learn even more. So that's why we write a series of nonfiction books that are companions to the fiction titles in the Magic Tree House® series. We call these books Fact Trackers because we love to track the facts! Whether we're researching dinosaurs, pyramids, Pilgrims, sea monsters, or cobras, we're always amazed at how wondrous and surprising the real world is. We want you to experience the same wonder we do—so get out your pencils and notebooks and hit the trail with us. You can be a Magic Tree House® Fact Tracker, too!

Here's what kids, parents, and teachers have to say about the Magic Tree House® Fact Trackers:

"They are so good. I can't wait for the next one. All I can say for now is prepare to be amazed!" —Alexander N.

"I have read every Magic Tree House book there is. The [Fact Trackers] are a thrilling way to get more information about the special events in the story." —John R.

"These are fascinating nonfiction books that enhance the magical time-traveling adventures of Jack and Annie. I love these books, especially *American Revolution*. I was learning so much, and I didn't even know it!" —Tori Beth S.

"[They] are an excellent 'behind-the-scenes' look at what the [Magic Tree House fiction] has started in your imagination! You can't buy one without the other; they are such a complement to one another." —Erika N., mom

"Magic Tree House [Fact Trackers] took my children on a journey from Frog Creek, Pennsylvania, to so many significant historical events! The detailed manuals are a remarkable addition to the classic fiction Magic Tree House books we adore!" —Jenny S., mom

"[They] are very useful tools in my classroom, as they allow for students to be part of the planning process. Together, we find facts in the [Fact Trackers] to extend the learning introduced in the fictional companions. Researching and planning classroom activities, such as our class Olympics based on facts found in *Ancient Greece and the Olympics*, help create a genuine love for learning!" —Paula H., teacher

MAGIC TREE HOUSE® FACT TRACKER

Leprechauns and Irish Folklore

A NONFICTION COMPANION TO MAGIC TREE HOUSE MERLIN MISSION #15:

Leprechaun in Late Winter

BY MARY POPE OSBORNE AND NATALIE POPE BOYCE

ILLUSTRATED BY SAL MURDOCCA

A STEPPING STONE BOOK™

Random House 🏠 New York

Visit us on the Web!
randomhousekids.com
MagicTreeHouse.com

Educators and librarians, for a variety of teaching tools, visit us at
RHTeachersLibrarians.com

Library of Congress Cataloging-in-Publication Data
Osborne, Mary Pope.
Leprechauns and Irish folklore : a nonfiction companion to Magic Tree House #43 :
Leprechaun in late winter / by Mary Pope Osborne and Natalie Pope Boyce ; illustrated
by Sal Murdocca.
p. cm. — (Magic tree house fact tracker)
Originally published : New York : Random House, c2010
"A Stepping Stone book." Includes index.
ISBN 978-0-375-86009-6 (trade) — ISBN 978-0-375-96009-3 (lib. bdg.) —
ISBN 978-0-307-97551-5 (ebook)
1. Leprechauns—Juvenile literature. 2. Fairies—Ireland—Juvenile literature.
3. Tales—Ireland—Juvenile literature. 4. Ireland—Folklore. I. Boyce, Natalie Pope.
II. Murdocca, Sal, ill. III. Osborne, Mary Pope. Leprechaun in late winter. IV. Title.
GR153.5.O753 2010 398.209417—dc22 2011000307

Printed in the United States of America
22 21

This book has been officially leveled by using the F&P Text Level Gradient™
Leveling System.

For Shan and Jack McCartie with love

Folklore Consultant:

LIAM HART, Irish language teacher and folk musician

Education Consultant:

HEIDI JOHNSON, Earth Science and Paleontology, Lowell Junior High School, Bisbee, Arizona

As always, very special thanks to the wonderful team at Random House: Gloria Cheng; Mallory Loehr; Liam Hart, who found our great photographs; Sal Murdocca, our wonderful artist; and especially to our editor, Diane Landolf.

LEPRECHAUNS
AND IRISH FOLKLORE

Contents

Dear Readers,

We spend a lot of time playing outdoors. We love to pretend that there are fairies living in the woods and gardens. We build fairy houses for them and make up stories about their adventures. We also like reading fairy stories. We've read fairy tales from all over the world, but the stories from Ireland are really exciting. Stories about the "wee folk" are in the heart and soul of Ireland.

We decided to learn about Irish folklore. We checked books out of the library and went online for more information. We found out that there are many kinds of Irish fairies in all shapes and sizes. We'd always heard

about leprechauns, but we never knew they were also fairies. Irish fairies can be scary, like the terrible dullahans and banshees, or playful, like the trooping fairies. Long ago many Irish people believed that fairies lived in the countryside and even in their houses! We wrote this book to introduce Irish fairies to you. So pack your bags and let's head to Ireland for an adventure with the wee folk.

Jack

Annie

1

🍀

Leprechauns and Irish Folklore

Ireland is an island near the coast of Great Britain. Because it rains a lot, Ireland is a very green country. It is so green that people call it the *Emerald Isle*. Emeralds are deep green stones that sparkle in the light. People often see rainbows shining over the green hills and valleys of the Emerald Isle.

There was a time in Ireland when many people believed in fairies. They claimed that on summer nights fairies danced in their gardens. When they saw clouds of dust blowing down the road, they said, "The fairies are riding their horses today." Even the rustling of leaves sounded like little fairy feet running through the woods.

Stories about fairies are an important part of Irish *folklore*. Folklore is the customs and stories of a people that are passed down through the years. Among the stories are tales of magical creatures that the Irish call the *wee folk*. The wee folk include tricky leprechauns and beautiful fairies that live in shining kingdoms under the hills.

Fairies are also called the "good folk" or the "gentle folk."

The Irish Oral Tradition

Many Irish fairy stories were first told by the *Celts* (KELTZ). The Celts came from

14

mainland Europe and settled in Ireland over two thousand years ago. Even though the Celts were mighty warriors, they loved to tell stories, recite poems, sing, and dance. They spoke an ancient language called Irish, or *Gaelic* (GAY-lik).

Today Irish storytellers are called
<u>seanachie</u> (SHAN-uh-kee), which means
"tellers of ancient tales."

Because the early Celts did not have books and did not write, they told stories to each other. Telling stories instead of reading them is called the *oral tradition.* For thousands of years, the oral tradition has played a large part in Irish culture. The Irish are famous the world over for their storytelling.

About sixteen hundred years ago, Christian monks and priests came to Ireland. They brought Christianity to the Irish Celts. The monks and priests also wrote down many old Celtic myths and stories. Their writings would later help people to research ancient Irish folklore.

The monks lived in places called <u>monasteries</u>. They were centers of learning and worship.

Stories in Danger

Most people in Ireland spoke Irish until about 150 years ago. The English ruled Ireland for many years. They wanted

16

Ireland to become more English and wanted to do away with old Irish customs. In 1871, the English made strict laws against the use of the Irish language. Children were punished if they spoke it in school. All signs and legal papers had to be in English.

English began to replace Irish as the most common language. It looked as if the language of the Celts would not survive. Because the old stories were in Irish, they, too, were in danger of fading away.

Douglas Hyde

Douglas Hyde was born in Ireland in 1860. When Douglas was a boy, he lived in the country. He often visited the cottage of an old gamekeeper named Seamus (SHAY-mus) Hart. Douglas loved to hear Seamus tell stories. Seamus told him about the adventures of mighty warriors, gods, and goddesses. He also told old Celtic tales about the wee folk, who had strange and magical powers.

Seamus died when Douglas was fourteen. Douglas was heartbroken.

Because of Seamus, Douglas wanted to learn all he could about his country's rich past. When he grew up, Douglas became a famous teacher of Irish folklore. But he knew that the old stories and the Irish language were in danger of slipping away forever.

To keep them alive, Douglas wrote

18

popular books about Irish folklore. He also urged people to speak Irish and to remember Irish music and dancing. In 1938, when Douglas was an old man, he became the first president of Ireland.

Douglas Hyde sits with his daughter and grandchildren.

Lady Gregory

Douglas Hyde had friends who also loved Irish folklore. One of them was Lady Augusta Gregory. Lady Gregory came from a rich family that lived in a large house in the country.

Lady Gregory

Lady Gregory's house was called Coole. The house is no longer standing, but you can visit the grounds and gardens.

Lady Gregory had a very happy childhood. She had fifteen brothers and sisters to play with! The children spent a lot of time in a garden that was filled with fruit trees and had strawberries growing along the paths. They roamed the countryside, explored the woods, and waded in the streams.

At night the children listened as their nurse, Mary Sheridan, told them old Irish folktales. Mary was an expert Irish speaker. Lady Gregory said that she held a whole library of Irish folklore in her head.

Lady Gregory at Work

Lady Gregory grew up and got married. After her husband died, she began to learn Irish and to research Irish folklore. She spent days reading old Celtic stories that the monks and priests had recorded many years before.

Lady Gregory also traveled the countryside, visiting cottages where people told her stories and talked about old customs and beliefs. She also went to shelters for the poor called workhouses. Lady Gregory sat with these folks for hours listening to their stories.

Lady Gregory later said she got her best stories from farmers, potato diggers, beggars, and poor people in the workhouse.

Like Douglas Hyde, Lady Gregory wrote books about Irish myths and fairy stories. She also wrote plays and gave speeches about Irish folklore. After many years of hard work, Lady Gregory died peacefully at Coole.

23

Besides Lady Gregory and Douglas Hyde, many other Irish speakers, writers, and storytellers helped to save their folklore. Thanks to all of them, Irish fairy stories, the Irish language, and all the other great tales from the past are safe.

A sign in both Irish and English for public restrooms.

What Are Fairies?

When the Celts became Christians, some legends say that their old gods and goddesses, called *Tuatha Dé Danann* (TOO-ha JAY DAN-uhn), changed themselves into fairies and went into hiding. Others claim that fairies were fallen angels who came to live on earth. They are said to live wherever they landed, in the water or on the land.

No matter where they came from, in Irish folklore there are two kinds of fairies. One kind is the *solitary* fairy. The word *solitary* means "living or being alone." Since leprechauns always live alone, they are solitary fairies.

The Irish word for fairies is <u>sí</u> (SHEE). This is also sometimes spelled <u>shee</u> or, the old Irish way, <u>sidhe</u>.

Fairies are supposed to live forever.

Other fairies live together. They are called the *trooping fairies*. The word *trooping* means "traveling together in groups." These fairies follow special trails called *fairy paths* when they move about. They also gallop down roads and across the fields on horseback. Most of the time, trooping fairies live in kingdoms deep under hills, in caves, or in rivers. Some even live in kingdoms deep under the seas.

Fairies do not trust humans and usually remain invisible. At times, however, people and fairies do come into contact. When this happens, the wee folk might be kind, or they might decide to make a whole lot of trouble. They like to play tricks on people, such as tripping them or making them sneeze. The fairies in the picture are busy changing a sign to confuse people.

Monks and the Filí

Many monks were gifted artists and writers. They lived simple lives, often in little stone huts or monasteries. Monks wrote on paper made from sheep or cow skin. They used different-colored inks to decorate their work.

The monks came into contact with powerful Celtic storytellers called the *filí*. The *filí* were men who trained for years to memorize Celtic history, stories, music, and poems. They were the ancient keepers of Celtic folklore. When the monks heard their stories, they wrote some of them down and decorated the pages with their art. Today you can still see some of these monks' beautiful work in museums and universities around the world.

2

Leprechauns and Other Solitary Fairies

The Emerald Isle is home to some of the most famous fairies in folklore. These fairies are the leprechauns. Leprechauns are solitary fairies who are never happier than when they are busy.

Leprechauns look like little old men. They dress in green and stand about three feet high. They wear pointed hats and shiny, buckled shoes. Tiny glasses perch firmly on their noses, and smoke from their smelly clay pipes fills the air around them.

A leprechaun working hard on fairy shoes.

Because leprechauns make the dainty shoes that other fairies love, they wear leather aprons with lots of pockets for their hammers and other tools.

Leprechauns are said to work under the shelter of leaves and hedges. Some people say that if you listen hard enough, you can sometimes hear the ringing of their hammers in the Irish countryside.

Keepers of the Treasure

There are many pictures of leprechauns standing beside pots of gold. Leprechauns are the richest of all the wee folk. They act as bankers and are very careful about lending their money to others. Stories say that they buried all the fairy gold for safekeeping when the Vikings invaded Ireland. From then on, it's been their job to guard it and keep it hidden.

The Vikings constantly raided this little monastery called Skellig Michael, which sits on a rock off the coast of Ireland.

There is a legend in Ireland that you will find gold at the end of the rainbow. That's a problem for leprechauns. If one of their

pots of gold lies under a rainbow, they have
to move it to another hiding place. Finding
new places keeps them very busy!

Tricky Little Guys

Leprechauns can be sneaky. If you manage to catch one, chances are you won't keep him very long. Once a leprechaun is captured, he'll promise to give you his money if you set him free.

It is really hard to get money from a leprechaun. He always carries two leather pouches around with him. One has a silver coin in it; the other has a gold coin. The leprechaun will promise to give both away if you set him free. If a person tries to collect the money, the silver coin always returns to the purse; the gold coin turns into ashes. And in the blink of an eye, the leprechaun vanishes.

Sometimes people try to trap leprechauns in their gardens. They put out little boxes with coins in them to lure the leprechaun inside. No one has ever reported finding a leprechaun in their box.

The Farmer and the Leprechaun

There is a story about a farmer who captured a leprechaun and forced him to reveal where he hid his gold. The leprechaun led the farmer to a field full of ragwort and pointed out one plant. "The gold is right here, under this plant," the leprechaun said.

Thinking he would soon be rich, the farmer tied a red cloth around the plant. Then he raced home for a shovel. When the farmer got back, he was shocked and angry. Every plant had a red cloth tied to it. To make matters worse, the leprechaun was nowhere in sight!

Clurichauns

Leprechauns have very lazy relatives called *clurichauns* (CLOOR-ih-konz). They are solitary fairies who look a lot like leprechauns. But unlike leprechauns, clurichauns enjoy dressing up. They wear red clothes, fancy blue silk stockings, and red caps with gold laces. Clurichauns also carry small bags of silver coins wherever they go.

Clurichauns really hate to work. Instead, they love to drink wine and have fun. At night they steal into rich people's cellars

These clurichauns are having fun by confusing a traveler.

and drink all their wine. They love wine so much that if the owner of the house drinks too many glasses, the clurichaun will sneak up and give him a good, hard pinch.

It's hard to get rid of clurichauns. If people move to a new house, they hide in a wine barrel and move right along with them.

Some folklore says that at night these fun-loving fairies like to take wild rides around the countryside on the backs of chickens, sheep, or sheepdogs.

Fear Dearg

The fear dearg (FARE JERR-ig) is also related to the leprechaun. Its name means "red man." These strange solitary

41

fairies have ugly yellow skin and dress in long red capes.

These fairies love to scare the wits out of everyone. They can make themselves look larger than they are. They can also make their voices sound like thunder or the roaring ocean. If a fear dearg gets bored, he plays jokes on people. He will kidnap someone and lock that person in a dark room. Then the fear dearg hides and makes horrible screaming and laughing sounds. Finally he lets his victims go.

Some people insist these wee folk are not really mean. They just enjoy playing pranks on people they like.

Let's go meet some other solitary fairies.

Banshees

Banshees are the fairies of death. They are said to wail outside the house of someone who is about to die. Banshees look like ghostly old women. They dress in gray and have long white hair. Their eyes are always red from crying for the dead.

At night banshees fly by the light of the moon or crouch behind trees. When they come to a house where someone is near death, they wail. Their wailing can sound sweet and low, or it can turn into terrible screams.

Long ago, many Irish women had the custom of *keening* together when a person died. *Keening* is another word for wailing. The sound of the women keening was thought to be like the wailing of the banshees.

Pookas

Pookas are wild spirits who come out at night. They live alone on high cliffs and

craggy mountaintops. Because pookas can change into many different animals, it's hard to recognize them. Sometimes they are soaring eagles, dogs, bulls, or goats. Much of the time, they are black horses with long tails and flowing manes. Blue flames shoot from their noses, filling the air with a nasty burning smell.

Pookas make superpowerful horses. They bound over hills and valleys, bellowing with human-like noises that can be heard from miles away. They uproot fields and knock down trees.

Sometimes pookas grab people and take them for wild horseback rides. When the pookas get tired of this game, they buck the people off. As the victims lie on the ground, they can hear the pookas chuckling as they slip back to their homes high in the hills.

Dullahans

Dullahans are super scary, really awful fairies. They appear as headless horsemen who gallop down dark roads. As they gallop, they carry their heads under their arms. Flames and sparks shoot from their huge black horses as the dullahans charge through the night. Stories say that they carry basins of blood with them to throw at everyone they see.

If that's not bad enough, dullahans have faces that are just horrifying. Their skin is like moldy old cheese, and they have enormous black mouths. Their terrible eyes dart around like insects.

Sometimes dullahans take banshees along with them and drive in black coaches pulled by six black headless horses. The coaches are covered in skulls and race down the road at breakneck speed. Legend says that when a dullahan's coach stops, some-one will die.

Merrows

Merrows are female fairies who live in beautiful kingdoms under the sea. Their name comes from the Irish words *múir* (MWIR), which means "sea," and *ógh* (OH), which means "maiden." Together these words mean the same as the English word *mermaid*.

Merrows have lower bodies like fish and upper bodies like beautiful women. Long hair flows down their backs, and they wear caps made of red feathers. Some merrows dress in sealskin cloaks. People say their cloaks and caps help them to swim like fish.

Merrows have haunting voices. They like to sit on the rocks and sing. If sailors hear their lovely music, they sometimes try to follow it and end up smashing their boats on the rocks. Merrows are said to be rich from the treasure they get from shipwrecks.

Merrows can live on land. But if they lose their caps, they can't return to the sea until they find them. When merrows cannot go back home, they often marry fishermen and have children. If they ever do find their caps, they will leave their families and return to their kingdoms in the sea.

Grogochs

Grogochs (GROH-goks) are the dirtiest fairies of all. If you hate baths, you are just like one! Grogochs look like tiny old men covered in red fur. They never bathe and wander around covered in leaves, twigs, and dirt. People are lucky that most of the time grogochs are invisible. Very few humans claim to have seen one.

According to Irish folklore, grogochs can live in both very cold and very hot weather. They make their homes in caves or under large, leaning stones. The Irish sometimes call stones that look like this grogoch houses.

If grogochs really like and trust people, they'll work in their kitchens. Sometimes they can be pests, and people trip over them. Other times, they are very helpful.

They scrub floors, wash dishes, and try to sweep. As a reward, the farm wife might give them a jug of rich, thick cream.

Ballybogs

Ireland has a lot of wetlands called peat bogs. Peat is formed when moss and other plants decay over thousands of years. The Irish burn peat in their fireplaces and put it in their gardens to help their plants grow. Bogs are so important that they have their own special fairies.

Ballybogs are fairies of the peat bog. They look very odd. Their little round bodies are covered in mud. They have no necks; their heads sit right on top of their bodies. They have very long, skinny arms and legs that are useless. Ballybogs cannot speak. Instead, they make grunting sounds and slobber a lot.

Ballybogs don't seem to be too bright. In fact, no one can figure out exactly what they do. Stories say they've been hanging around bogs for hundreds of years. If you like bogs, ballybogs are your kind of wee folk!

3

♣

Trooping Fairies

Trooping fairies build their kingdoms in hills near the ruins of old Celtic forts. Stories say that if you walk nine times around a fairy hill during a full moon, you will find the entrance to a fairy kingdom. Deep inside the hill is a fairy palace with crystal walls that sparkle like diamonds.

Fairies love beautiful things. Rooms in their palaces are painted in rich colors like red, green, and gold. Elegant rugs lie on golden floors, and fine furniture fills the rooms. The fairies feast in a special dining room with diamond walls. Flickering candles light the room while the fairies dine on honey, cakes, and milk.

Fairies love to stand on leaves and sip the nectar from flowers.

What Do They Look Like?

Trooping fairies look like small, beautiful people and have long golden hair. They even act a little like humans. They love to dance and sing. They fall in love, get married, and have children. They also fight, play tricks on people, get angry, and have their own holidays.

Each fairy kingdom has its own king and queen. The queens and princesses are said to wear sparkling green or white gowns with pearls and gold sewed onto them. The kings and princes dress in green and wear red hats with gold ribbons woven into them. They also wear heavy gold necklaces called *torcs*. Other fairies also wear pretty, shiny clothes, usually in soft green, white, or gray. Some wear capes and pointed caps.

Celtic kings also wore torcs.

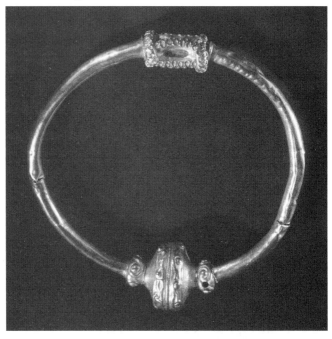

Folklore says that these wee fairy folk can fly as fast as the wind. They change themselves into different shapes and sizes and make themselves invisible when they don't want to be seen.

Fairies often ride horses through the

fields and down the lanes. With their special magic, they can change cabbage leaves and weeds into prancing steeds. They braid the horses' tails and manes and decorate their saddles. Fairy horses are beautiful and strong and charge over ditches and fences at breakneck speeds. Stories say that at night fairies often ride their horses on their way to dances with other fairies. Dust swirls around them as they race down the country lanes. Some folks claim they sound like a swarm of bees as they gallop along.

Fairy horses are so fast that they can gallop around the world and ride moonbeams all in one night.

Trooping Fairies

Small

Look like humans

Live forever

Can be invisible

Live in kingdoms under the hills

Fairy Mischief

Sometimes fairies cause a bit of trouble. One thing that they really like is fighting with other groups of fairies. During a battle, they whack each other over the heads with blackthorn sticks. (Don't try this with your friends!) It's said that many a poor farmer has found his potato field in ruins after a fairy fight.

Stories tell of fairies perching on rooftops to watch the folks below. They like to spy on people celebrating or going about their business on the farms and in the fields.

Only a fairy doctor can cure the spell from a fairy dart.

If a farmer forgets to leave extra grain in his fields for the fairies, they sometimes shoot fairy darts at him or his cows. The darts make it impossible for the victim to move until the spell is undone.

Fairies like to slip into barns and steal milk from the cows. Then they kick over the milk buckets. Fairies can also make eggs disappear from right under the hens and will pull the cat's tail.

If that's not enough mischief, the frisky
fairies will make tangles in people's hair and

Protection Against Fairy Mischief

Leave an offering of
a little honey cake on
your windowsill.

Fairies hate mess. Stay
tidy . . . sweep out your
fireplace.

Wear your coat inside out.

Carry around a branch
of rowanberries.

steal little things like eyeglasses and keys and bigger things like horses and children!

Nail a horseshoe over your door.

Draw a pig's head on your door.

Put a sock under your bed.

Ring church bells.

Fairies Doing Good

At times, the wee folk help people. Stories say that when fields get too dry and the crops begin to die, fairies will cause a good rain to fall. Sometimes they even harvest crops and build houses for farmers who are in trouble.

Fairies also act as doctors to humans. Legends say that fairies study medicine and are experts at healing. They use prayers, chanting, and herbs to treat a sick person. Fairy doctors will never take money for curing someone. They will, however, accept gifts.

Some fairy doctors were believed to have taught their skills to human women. In this picture, fairies are dancing with a woman named Ann Jeffries. Long ago, many believed Ann had learned the art of healing from fairy doctors.

The Cottingley Fairies

In 1917, two English schoolgirls caused great excitement. They were cousins named Elsie Wright and Frances Griffiths. The girls claimed to have taken pictures of fairies in a place called Cottingley Glen. They had photographs of themselves next to beautiful winged fairies. Experts looked at the pictures. Many said that they seemed real and believed the girls' story.

Years later, when Elsie and Frances were old women, they confessed that it was all a prank. They had cut out pictures of fairies from a book and posed beside them. Even today, people visit Cottingley Glen hoping to see fairies dancing there. They still can't believe that Elsie and Frances were just playing a joke.

Cottingley fairies

4

🍀

Fairy Places

In 1999, a group of engineers stood in a field next to a hawthorn tree. An Irish story-teller named Eddie Lenihan was with them. Eddie had to warn the men against building a highway through the field. He explained that destroying the hawthorn would make the fairies angry. Hawthorns are special fairy trees.

Eddie told the engineers that the fairies would be so angry that they would cause

Eddie Lenihan may be Ireland's most famous storyteller.

people to wreck their cars if the road were ever built. Eddie won the argument. The engineers changed their plans and built the highway around the field. The hawthorn was saved.

There are many fairy places like this field in Ireland. Douglas Hyde once said that every tree, hill, and valley in Ireland has its own strange and wonderful tales.

Trees and Bushes

Fairy folklore about special trees can be traced back to the beliefs of the ancient Celts. The Celts thought that certain places and certain trees were *sacred*.

Sacred means "holy and respected."

The oak tree was their most sacred tree. Celtic wise men called *Druids* held many of their ceremonies in groves of oak trees.

People used to say that "fairy folks are in old oaks." Legend says that just like the Druids did, fairies honor the oak, the hawthorn, and a small tree called the rowan tree, or mountain ash.

Rowan trees have strong branches that make good walking sticks.

People often tied ribbons to the branches of these trees, hoping that the fairies would send them good luck. There was a belief that anyone who harmed a special fairy tree was in big trouble!

Ribbons are tied to a hawthorn tree in County Meath, Ireland.

The Irish used to place branches of red rowanberries in their doorways to please the fairies. They also hung hawthorn in their barns in hopes of getting more milk from their cows.

The Fairies' Revenge

There is a tale of a man who wanted to saw down a rowan tree. As he began his work, he spotted smoke in the distance. It was coming from his cottage. The man raced home, but when he got there, the fire had gone out by itself. This happened several more times.

Finally the man thought it was safe to continue cutting down the tree, and he did. That evening he returned home, only to find that his house had burned to the ground. The fairies had their revenge!

It is said that if people fall asleep under fairy trees, they will wake up in a fairy kingdom.

Fairy Paths

Animals are said to avoid walking on fairy paths.

Fairy paths are supposed to run across all of Ireland. Folklore says that the paths are straight and even go under lakes and rivers. They connect fairy places to each other. The fairies use the paths for daily fairy business. They also travel on them to battle with other fairy tribes, or just for friendly visits.

Fairies trooping down a fairy path on their way to a dance.

If people build their houses on a fairy path, the fairies get very angry. Sometimes they throw the furniture outside or keep the owners up all night with the sound of marching fairy feet. Only the fairies know where the paths are, which makes it hard for people to figure out where it is safe to build.

Lady Gregory wrote that people said a house was "in the way" when residents had lots of bad luck.

Lanty's New House

There is a famous Irish story about a farmer named Lanty M'Cluskey. Lanty had just gotten married. He built a house for his new wife. Everyone warned him that the house was on a fairy playground. Lanty would not pay attention. When he completed the house, Lanty hired a fiddler and invited all of his neighbors over for a party.

It began to get dark, and everyone was having fun dancing and laughing. Suddenly a crushing, crashing noise came from the top of Lanty's house. It sounded as if the wood was splintering and the top of the house was being torn apart. Everyone stopped and listened.

Then they heard the sound of a thousand little fairy voices straining and groaning as if they were pushing on something. "Hurry up," one voice said. "Work hard; we have to have Lanty's house down by midnight."

Lanty was stunned. Fairies were destroying his house! He told them he was sorry. He promised to pull the house down himself the next morning.

The guests heard the sounds of a thousand pairs of little hands clapping and tiny voices shouting, "Bravo, Lanty! Build your new house between the two thorn trees above the road!" Then the fairies vanished into the night.

Lanty did as he had promised. When he dug the foundation for his new house, he found that the fairies had left him a bit of gold as a special gift.

Solving the Problem

Over the years, people did certain things to solve the building problem. Sometimes they put four stones where they wanted the corners of a house to be. If the stones were still in place and not scattered around the next

morning, it meant that it was all right to
build on that spot.

Other people believed that if they threw a hat in the air, it was safe to put a house wherever the hat landed.

 People also got advice from "wise women" like Peig Sayers, who were experts on fairies and their ways.

If people did have their house on a fairy track, they would try to please the fairies. Sometimes they put buckets of water out for the fairies to drink as they passed through. They also cut off any part of the house that lay on the path.

There are old Irish houses still standing with their corners lopped off.

Since fairies traveled in straight lines, people often tried to line up their front and back doors so that the fairies could troop straight through the house.

Fairy Circles and Forts

The Celts lived in round forts called *raths* (RAHZ). They piled up mounds of dirt or rocks around the raths for protection. The raths fell into ruins long ago. Today all that is left of most of them is a circle of stones where they once stood. Thousands of these old stone rings dot the Irish

Celts also built forts on islands in lakes. These forts are called crannogs.

Stone rath

countryside. Some people say there are the remains of over 3,000 ring forts in Ireland.

Folklore has it that fairies make their homes in the hills under the ruins. They guard these sites carefully. People would be wise to stay away.

Stories say that magic sometimes happens at the fairies' ring forts. On moonlit nights, especially in the spring, the fairies are supposed to dance in the circles. There

are said to be miles of fairy tunnels running under the ruins and fairy kingdoms hidden deep inside.

In the past, farmers were careful not to disturb raths and crannogs. Legend says that if anyone trespassed on fairy places, the fairies would cause them to have accidents or get sick. The fairies might even turn them into animals like owls or rabbits!

There's a rabbit under that bush! I bet it was once a mean farmer who destroyed a rath!

Oh, Annie, that's just a story.

Druids and Special Places

Fairy legends about sacred places may have come from the Druids. Druids trained for many years as priests, teachers, judges, and doctors. They believed that gods and goddesses lived in everything in nature. To them every rock, hill, plant, and animal had a living spirit inside it. They called this spirit world the Otherworld.

Druids honored natural things such as trees, plants, water, and certain hills. They claimed that waterfalls were the door to the Otherworld. They held ceremonies in oak and ash groves. In their rituals, the Druids often used branches of mistletoe or holly. They also thought that certain wells, streams, and lakes had powers to heal the sick.

The Druids left little offerings to their gods and goddesses in the hollows of trees or behind rocks . . . just like the gifts people often left for fairies.

5

♣

Fairy Dancing and Music

Fairies enjoy music, dancing, and feasting. Legend says that fairy music is so haunting that it can change a person's life forever. There is a story of a man who visited an old Irish cottage. In the corner, a young girl sat by the fire, chanting the same sad song over and over again. She did not notice anything around her and seemed to be in a world of her own.

When the man asked what was wrong

with the girl, he was told that she had once heard a fairy harp. Its soft music put her in a trance. The girl lost her memory and could no longer hear any sound but the fairy harp.

People thought that if the spell was broken, the girl would die. Even today, if an Irish girl is caught daydreaming, people say, "She is away with the fairies."

Fairy music is supposed to be the most wonderful sound in the world. Fairy musicians play harps, fiddles, pipes, and drums. Sometimes the music is haunting and sweet; other times it's lively and makes the fairies dance until they wear out their tiny shoes.

Today Irish musicians still play the same instruments that the fairies supposedly play. All through the ages, the

Irish have been great music makers. There are stories that even the fairies love listening to Irish music. Sometimes they hide in the rafters and listen to the music at weddings and other celebrations. Other times, people catch glimpses of them dancing on the nearby hills.

The ancient Celts also loved music and played the Irish harp. It's the national symbol of Ireland.

The Fairies and Turlough O'Carolan

Folklore says that if a good musician falls asleep on a fairy ring fort, that person will wake up with the gift of fairy music. This is said to have happened to a blind harper and poet

O'Carolan

named Turlough O'Carolan. He was a real person who lived in Ireland in the 1600s. O'Carolan is one of the most beloved harpers that Ireland ever had.

Every year harpers hold a celebration for O'Carolan. They play their harps and visit his grave.

Legend has it that one night O'Carolan fell asleep on a fairy fort. As he slept, the fairies sent their music so deeply into his dreams that when O'Carolan woke up, he remembered it note for note. From then on, his playing was filled with magic.

92

O'Carolan went all over Ireland playing his harp. There is a story that once when he visited some friends, he found them crying. They were heartbroken because fairies had stolen their baby. To comfort them, O'Carolan played a beautiful song on his harp. The fairies were so moved by it that they returned the child to its parents.

Several fairy tunes are said to survive. "Pretty Girl Milking Her Cow" is one of them.

Fairies sometimes kidnapped babies right out of their cribs.

Dancing

On clear nights, fairies come out to dance in the moonlight. Most of the time, they dance in circles on the raths. But they are also said to dance under hawthorn trees and in round grass circles called fairy rings. As their music fills the air, the fairies form a circle. Then they hold hands and begin to dance.

Fairy rings are circles in the grass caused by a fungus. Mushrooms often grow around the circle.

People who come across them are often drawn in by the music. It casts a spell that makes them dance until they can hardly stand up. Even when they want to, the people cannot stop dancing. When the sun comes up, the fairies vanish. By then, the poor people are so exhausted they fall into a heap on the ground and sleep.

The Girl and the Fairy Dance

There is a story about a pretty girl who found herself dancing with a fairy prince. The music and the dance were like a beautiful dream.

Afterward the prince invited the girl to his fairy kingdom. There was a table waiting for them, set with plates of gold and silver. The prince offered the girl a sip of wine from a golden goblet. Before she could take

a drink, someone whispered, "Do not eat or drink. If you do, you'll never return home."

The girl became so frightened that she almost fainted. Suddenly a redheaded man took her hand and led her out. He pressed a branch of ivy into her hand. "This will keep you safe," he promised.

As the girl raced home, she could hear fairy footsteps thundering behind her. She quickly locked her door and went to bed. All through the night, tiny voices could be heard outside yelling, "Come back! Next time when you dance to our music on the hill, you'll stay with us forever and no one will help you!"

The girl held on to the magic branch of ivy with all her might and woke up in her bed the next day. The fairies never bothered her again. But memories of the beautiful dance haunted her forever.

Halloween

The ancient Celts set aside the first night of November to honor the dead. They knew that winter was coming and that the days would soon get shorter and darker. It was a gloomy time as the Celts got ready to face the cold days ahead.

They believed that on November 1, the spirits of the dead rose from the grave and roamed the earth. They also believed that ghosts, fairies, and witches came out on this scary night. To help the spirits find their way in the dark, the Celts burned bonfires on the hills.

According to legend, fairies celebrated November 1 in much the same way.

Dullahans, pookas, and all sorts of scary fairies are said to be on the lookout for victims that night. Today we celebrate Halloween at the same time of year. Our custom has its roots in the ancient world of the Celts.

6

Where Are the Fairies?

Stories say that at one time more fairies lived in Ireland than people. The fairies all spoke Irish. As the Irish language faded, the fairies began to disappear. It's thought that those who remain stay in their kingdoms deep inside the green hills. Some folks say that many fairies moved to distant islands or high up in the lonely mountains.

In Irish folklore, there is a land called Tír na nÓg (CHEER nuh NOHG). Tír na

means "land
of the ever-
young."

nÓg is an enchanted world where no one
ever grows old or dies. It is said to be

Fairies are heading for the beautiful
land of Tír na nÓg.

home to many fairies and the Tuatha Dé Danann, who were the old gods and goddesses of the Celts. A snow-white fairy horse carries the fairies there.

Some say Tír na nÓg is an island far away in the ocean. The sky is always blue there, and the winds are always gentle. Others say Tír na nÓg lies beneath the sea, removed from the world of troubles and worry. According to Irish folklore, the only way a person can get to Tír na nÓg is to be invited by a fairy. The fairies love this magic land where they stay forever young and beautiful.

But fairies live somewhere else as well—in the books we read and the stories we tell about them. Even though today most Irish claim not to believe in fairies, they admit that the spirit of the fairies is still in their hearts.

Irish folklore will probably be around for a very long time. It has played a big part in making the Irish who they are today. And who knows whether the wee

folk really exist or where they really are? Maybe fairies are living in your garden right now as you read this book about their magical lives.

Doing More Research

There's a lot more you can learn about leprechauns and Irish folklore. The fun of research is seeing how many different sources you can explore.

Books

Most libraries and bookstores have lots of books about Irish folklore.

Here are some things to remember when you're using books for research:

1. You don't have to read the whole book. Check the table of contents and the index to find the topics you're interested in.

2. Write down the name of the book. When you take notes, make sure you write

down the name of the book in your note-book so you can find it again.

3. Never copy exactly from a book.
When you learn something new from a book, put it in your own words.

4. Make sure the book is nonfiction or has old, traditional stories.
Some books tell new, make-believe stories about leprechauns and Irish fairies. Make-believe stories are called *fiction*. They're fun to read, but not good for research.

Research books have facts and tell true stories. They are called *nonfiction*. Books of folklore have old stories that have been passed down through the years. A librarian or teacher can help you make sure the books you use for research are non-fiction or folklore.

Here are some good books of Irish folklore:

- *Favorite Celtic Fairy Tales* by Joseph Jacobs

- *Favorite Fairy Tales Told in Ireland* by Virginia Haviland

- *Irish Fairy Tales* edited by Philip Smith

- *A Pot o' Gold: A Treasury of Irish Stories, Poetry, Folklore, and (of Course) Blarney* by Kathleen Krull

- *The Prince of Ireland and the Three Magic Stallions* by Bryce Milligan

- *Tales from Old Ireland* by Malachy Doyle

DVDs

There are some great DVDs about Irish history, mythology, and folklore. As with books, make sure the DVDs you watch for research are nonfiction!

Check your library or video store for these and other nonfiction titles about Irish folklore:

- *The Celts: Rich Traditions and Ancient Myths*
  from BBC Video

- *In Search of Ancient Ireland*
  from PBS

- *Irish Myths & Legends*
  from Delta

The Internet

Many websites have lots of information about Irish folklore. Some also have games and activities that can help make learning about Irish folklore even more fun.

Ask your teacher or your parents to help you find more websites like these:

• apples4theteacher.com/holidays /st-patricks-day/short-stories

• ehow.com/how_4824360_identify-fairies -other-wee-folk.html

• irelandseye.com/animation/intro.html

• www.shee-eire.com/Magic&Mythology /Fairylore/main.htm

• timelessmyths.com/celtic/faeries.html

Good luck!

Index

*Have you read the adventure that
matches up with this book?*

Don't miss
Magic Tree House® Merlin Mission #15

LEPRECHAUN IN LATE WINTER

The magic tree house whisks Jack and Annie
to nineteenth-century Ireland. There
they meet an Irish girl and go on a magical
adventure that changes her life!

If you like Magic Tree House® Merlin Mission #16:

A Ghost Tale for Christmas Time,

you'll love finding out the facts behind the fiction in

Magic Tree House® Fact Tracker

Rags and Riches:

Kids in the Time of Charles Dickens

A NONFICTION COMPANION TO **A Ghost Tale for Christmas Time**

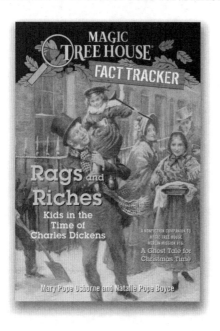

It's Jack and Annie's very own
guide to Victorian kids!

Available now!

Enough cool facts
to fill a tree house!

Jack and Annie have been all over the world in their adventures in the magic tree house. And they've learned lots of incredible facts along the way. Now they want to share them with you! Get ready for a collection of the weirdest, grossest, funniest, most all-around amazing facts that Jack and Annie have ever encountered. It's the ultimate fact attack!

Magic Tree House®

Magic Tree House® Merlin Missions

Magic Tree House®
Super Edition

Magic Tree House®
Fact Trackers

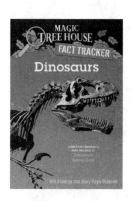

More Magic Tree House®